COMPANIONS
on
My Journey

Kathy McInnis

ISBN 978-1-64349-189-9 (paperback)
ISBN 978-1-64349-190-5 (digital)

Christian Faith Publishing, Inc.
832 Park Avenue
Meadville, PA 16335
www.christianfaithpublishing.com

The Bible. English Standard Version, Crossway, 2008.
The Bible. New English Translation, Biblical Studies Press, 2005.
The Bible. New International Version, Zondervan, 1984.
The Bible. King James Version.

Printed in the United States of America

He who sees God as angry does not see him rightly but looks only on a curtain, as if a dark cloud had been drawn across his face.
—Martin Luther

Introduction

God created each of us for his purpose. We are in this place at this time to fulfill that purpose. I have stumbled; I have fallen. My scars are testimonies to God's infinite grace and mercy. The purpose in sharing my faith-journey is to offer encouragement and solace to those who may be struggling with fear, shame, depression, or unbelief. God stitched my pain, my mistakes, and my brokenness into the tapestry of his incredible love story. May you be inspired to turn to the Creator God who loves you eternally.

When I was a teenager, my mom told me that I walked around with a cloud over my head. She had no idea the truth in her statement, neither did she know the heavy weight of that dark cloud. The cloud cast deep shadows over every area of my life. Hiding in those shadows were sinister companions that would stalk me for years.

This book, *Companions on My Journey*, is an attempt to share my messy journey through the darkness into the marvelous light of God's love and grace. At the cross, I found healing and peace, freedom and restoration. I pray that my Heavenly Father will use my story to guide the hurting, the rejected, the abused, and the condemned into the miraculous light of his unfathomable love. Please take my hand and journey with me.

Prologue

December 25, 1984, is my last day on earth. Drowning in pain, the pressure in my chest is an anvil against my ribs. I gulp down air. "Why is my heart still beating?" As I collapse to the floor of an empty apartment, I wonder what has led me to this place of utter despair. I am only twenty-five years old; my life should not be ending this way.

What unforgiveable sin have I committed to deserve such pain? At what point in my relatively short life have I gone off-script? As far back as I can remember, I have been a rule-follower. I have been unrelenting in my continual pursuit of perfection. What unwritten rule have I broken? "This isn't supposed to be happening to me," I whimper as I lose consciousness.

The Fear of the Lord

During most of my childhood, the mountains of east Tennessee were my home. Romping through the woods, climbing trees, and building forts with my brothers were my favorite past times. Having both sets of grandparents living nearby was a special blessing. Dad's parents lived across the cow pasture. Mom's parents lived about three or four miles down a gravel road. My siblings and I took turns spending Friday nights with each set of grandparents. I suspected my grandparents were rich because they had indoor bathrooms.

The only plumbing in our tiny house was in the kitchen where ice-cold water was pumped from a well. Our toilet was in a rustic brown building standing at the end of a dirt path. We didn't have the luxury of standing under a nice, hot shower every morning; we didn't have a shower. Our bathtub was an oval steel feeding trough hanging on the back porch, which my dad brought into the kitchen on Saturday nights for our weekly baths. Throughout the week, we took *sponge baths* in the kitchen sink.

We were poor, but we had plenty of food. Dad planted a beautiful garden every year, and Mom canned most of what was harvested. We enjoyed fresh eggs from our chickens and consumed unpasteurized milk from our cow. Mom churned our butter.

My childhood wasn't complicated, except for the spiritual part. The beginning of my spiritual journey was a little rocky and laid the foundation for spiritual dysfunction that would follow me for many years. Whether my heart was born with a sense of condemnation or whether it had been wounded early by toxic religion, thoughts of God always filled my little heart with fear. The joyless Christians surrounding me exacerbated my faulty view of God. He was an old, cranky gentleman that sat above the clouds just waiting to damn sinners to hell. In Sunday school, I was taught that God was love and that he sent Jesus to die for my sins. If that was true, why did the preacher constantly yell about an angry god?

My insides shuddered as I observed the solemn faces of everyone taking communion on Sunday mornings. Crawling onto my dad's lap and hiding my face in his chest was protection against whatever might be lurking in those sacred elements.

I was ten years old when I followed my cousin down the church's aisle as she responded to the invitation. I really didn't know what I was doing. She was crying, and I was drawn to follow. Mom and Dad joined me as I knelt beside my cousin. Mom was sobbing. Dad was shouting. I was embarrassed. I wasn't sure why there was such a fuss.

When the preacher asked if I feared the Lord, my internal response was "Of course, I fear the Lord. He scares me to death." Instead, I answered, "Yes, sir." My mom said something to the congregation, which shocked me because she was extremely shy. I just felt strange and wanted to get out of there as soon as possible.

One week later, I was baptized in the icy waters of Gobey Creek. There was shouting and praying and singing. Yet I was more concerned about not freezing to death or having a salamander crawl up my leg. I don't think that was the proper attitude of a new Christian.

A few months after my thirteenth birthday, my dad announced his call to full-time ministry. We left the little country church and moved our membership to a church in town. Wearing pants was forbidden for women, and makeup was sorely frowned upon. My mother took pity on me because of my rosacea and allowed me to wear makeup sparingly. As a Christian, being a rule-follower was my number one priority. Otherwise, I might antagonize the angry god.

Fear and Anger

In 1972 our family of seven moved from east Tennessee to the city of Greenville, South Carolina so my dad could attend seminary. I was a miserable teenager. I did not like the city. I felt like an orchid plucked out of paradise and placed in a petri dish. Concrete and buildings replaced my beautiful mountains and trees.

I was fourteen when I started babysitting the children of our church's associate pastor. Cleaning the house was also one of my responsibilities. While making the bed one morning, I was listening to a fire-and-brimstone preacher on the radio (I'm not sure why this was my station of choice). As I smoothed the wrinkles from the bedspread, fear and dread suddenly surged through my soul. I realized that I might not really be a Christian. Fear of dying and going to hell was overwhelming. Falling on my knees, I asked God to save me. Again, I feared God.

The next few years were spent working to pay tuition to attend our church's Christian school. While the place called itself a Christian school, it felt more like a boot camp training me in the art of perfectionism. An internal compulsion drove me to never disappoint my parents or the leaders of my church. Anything other than straight As was unacceptable. As a cheerleader and a member of the student council, I was popular and well-liked. Yet secretly I carried a constant sense of dread that someone might discover I was hollow inside.

Dad accepted the call to pastor a small church in Virginia at the end of my junior year of high school. Dread flooded my heart as

I thought about leaving my small group of friends and moving to a city where I knew no one. I begged my parents to allow me to stay with the family next door, but my parents refused. For many years, I harbored anger toward my parents and especially toward God.

My New Companions

The school in Virginia was a large public school. The other students thought I was a little weird. I was the preacher's kid who always wore dresses and never smiled. My only redeeming qualities were extremely long hair and a shapely figure. Burying myself in my studies helped drown out the sneering, and graduating second in my class vindicated my perceived weirdness.

In the summer of 1977, I fell in love. Unfortunately, I made the mistake of falling in love with a man who was divorced. It didn't matter that his wife left him for another man; divorce was one of the unpardonable sins. Instead of the scarlet letter *A* on his chest, many believed a flaming *D* should have been branded on his forehead.

One weekend that summer, my parents went out of town and left me and one of my brothers behind. My brother and I made plans to go along with several friends to a carnival. I was supposed to ride with my brother, but plans changed and the ride was no longer available. Then, *the love of my life* showed up and offered to drive me. In my naïveté, I accepted his offer.

When he picked me up, I was bubbling with anticipation. We stopped at the main intersection in town, and an oil can rolled from the back of his car up under his feet. I leaned down to remove the can so it wouldn't interfere with his driving. He and I were unaware that one of the women in my dad's church was standing on the corner. She saw us.

Word spread like wildfire that the preacher's daughter was running away with the divorcee. A friend met us at the carnival and warned us about the rumor. Terror engulfed me as I thought of what my parents would do once they heard the rumors. The rumors were repugnant, but there had been no ungodly actions between me and my love. Truthfully, I was just an eighteen-year-old girl who had accepted a ride from a man whose unpardonable sin was being divorced.

Within minutes of my parents return, the love of my life arrived to talk with my father. Sitting at my bedroom window, I strained to overhear the conversation. I could not hear their words, but the tone seemed friendly. As he was leaving, my love looked toward my bedroom window with a deep sadness in his eyes.

My dad called me down to the living room, but I was not allowed to give my side of the story. I had humiliated the family and disgraced the church. My mother asked what was wrong with me. I had no idea how to answer that.

The next morning, my father drove me to the house of the woman who had been standing on the corner. Forced to apologize to her for being such a wayward young woman, fear, shame, and condemnation became my persistent companions.

Disappointment and Guilt

In the fall of 1977, I left home to attend a very conservative Christian university in South Carolina. The environment of legalism proved to be a greenhouse of dysfunction. My fear, shame, and condemnation began to grow exponentially. Innumerable unwritten rules weighed heavily on my tormented soul. In this toxic environment, I met my future husband.

He was handsome, charming, confident, and everything I was not. He was an artist and studying to go into full-time ministry. We both felt as if we had met our soul mates, so we made plans to marry. Unfortunately, two broken souls do not make a whole.

I attended college on a work scholarship program. Near the end of my second year, I visited the dean of finance to ask if I should take off a semester and earn more money to put toward my tuition balance. He assured me that everything was fine and I could rest easy.

A week before leaving school for summer break, I gathered the courage to go to the dean of biblical studies and ask about one of the doctrinal standings taught by the college. The dean was quite shocked that I would be so bold as to ask questions. The meeting did not go well.

Summer break of 1979 seemed shorter than usual. Two weeks prior to returning to college, I received a letter from the university stating that I would need to pay the balance of my tuition before arriving for my junior year. I was unable to return to college that fall.

While working and saving money, I prayed I would be able to complete my college education. During that time, unrest in our church boiled over, and Dad resigned as pastor. He was left penniless and borrowed money from one of my uncles so the family could move back to Tennessee.

Guilt became a familiar companion when I was unable to find a job in Tennessee. I believed I was a financial burden to my family, so moving up my wedding plans seemed a logical escape. My future husband was working as a youth pastor in Georgia. Dad didn't trust my future husband, but he didn't stop me from leaving. After all, my departure would lighten the financial burden.

In Georgia I found a job right away and moved in with a family from the church where my future husband was working. This family was so kind me, and I experienced unconditional love for the first time in many years. The joy and laughter in their home was a soothing balm to my tortured soul.

Two weeks prior to our wedding, I noticed jealousy and strange bouts of pouting from my future husband. Something just didn't feel right, but my own insecurity hindered my ability to recognize my unease as a warning. One Sunday evening, he flew into a jealous tirade. Shaking, I ran from the house. After calming down, I stood at the edge of the yard staring at the long winding road, wondering if I was making a terrible mistake. For a second I thought about going back home to Tennessee, but shame and guilt engulfed my heart. I could not go back. My toxic companions grew stronger.

Constant Companions

Our wedding was simple but pretty. Still reeling from the financial devastation of a few months prior, my parents could not attend the wedding. I met my father-in-law for the first time. He was a handsome man with a gorgeous laugh and a loving spirit. He and my husband's mother had been divorced for several years. She was unable to attend the wedding because of the illness of her current husband.

Only a few days into our honeymoon, I realized that my marriage was not going to be one of those happily-ever-after stories in fairy tales. My new husband, a youth pastor, was emotionally, physically, and mentally abusive. We were supposed to be a young, happy Christian couple. That was a lie. Grappling to make sense of my situation, fear of my husband supplanted my fear of God.

Six months after our honeymoon, my husband decided that we should move to Texas to be closer to his family. I could not protest; I was not allowed an opinion.

We arrived in Texas in October 1980, and I met my mother-in-law for the first time. She was a beautiful woman with a contagious smile. Instinctively, I knew I could talk to her about anything, but I was not prepared for her brutal honesty.

During an evening walk, my mother-in-law stopped, put her arms around me, and stared into my eyes. "I wish I had been able to meet you before you married my son. I know this will frighten you, but your life with him is going to be a living hell. Please know that I will always be here for you no matter what. I will do my best to protect you from my son." I was shocked to the core. I stood there with my mouth open not knowing how to respond. I had only known this woman a couple of hours. We walked back to her house in silence.

The months passed, and I accepted that I could do nothing to please my husband. We were married ten months when I discovered that I was pregnant with twins. Leaving the doctor's office, I rushed home to tell my husband. I was so excited; maybe being a father would make him happy.

Arriving at the apartment, I gushed with the news that we were going to have twins. He looked at me with utter contempt, "You have got to be kidding me!" He walked into our bedroom, slammed the door, and left me standing alone.

I slept on the couch that night and cried myself to sleep.

"Why, God? Why is this happening? What did I do wrong? Why doesn't he love me? Why doesn't he want children? God, what have I done to deserve this?"

I went into labor six weeks early. My doctor put me on bedrest hoping to slow down the progress. The ultrasound showed that the twins only weighed two or three pounds. However, a week of bedrest did not slow down the progression of labor. The twins were born five weeks early. During delivery, I wondered if the look of surprise on the doctor's face was cause for concern. Fortunately, once my first-born's body was free of her constraints, one of the nurses laughed. "Those are no three-pound babies!" Christina weighed six pounds and four ounces. Carolyn weighed five pounds eight ounces. Thank God they were born early!

As the twins grew, so did my husband's anger. He turned his anger away from me and toward our daughters. I went to the leaders of our church begging for help. They admonished me to be a more submissive wife. How much more submissive could I be? I was melting into an invisible person. My thoughts were not my own; my words were not my own. I wasn't sure who I was. The church leaders respectfully advised my husband that joining an extracurricular activity like baseball would relieve his stress. Fear, shame, and condemnation became my constant companions.

Facing Death

Recognizing fear in the eyes of my precious daughters began shaking me from my victim mentality. They were toddlers when my husband's slap left a handprint on Christina's little face. Knowing the church would not offer sanctuary, I called my husband's father and brother and begged for help. While my father-in-law reasoned with my husband, my brother-in-law took me and my daughters into his home. After assurances that the abuse would stop, the twins and I moved back in with my husband. Within weeks, the abuse turned back on me. Paralyzing fear chained me to a life of pain.

After four years of marriage, my husband started seeing another woman. Part of me should have felt relief. Instead, rejection joined my expanding crowd of companions.

I drove my daughters to my parents in Tennessee and asked them to take the twins for a few weeks while I attempted to save my marriage. I prayed. I cried. I prayed some more, but my prayers bounced off the ceiling. I tried everything within my power to save whatever shred of hope might be left in this so-called marriage. Divorce was not an option; it was one of the unforgiveable sins to avoid at all costs. Finally, alone and broken, death whispered its soothing refrain.

December 25, 1984, was my last day on earth. Drowning in pain, the pressure in my chest was an anvil against my ribs. I gulped down air. "Why is my heart still beating?" As I collapsed to the floor of an empty apartment, I wondered what had led me to this place of utter despair. I was only twenty-five years old; my life should not be ending this way.

What unforgiveable sin had I committed to deserve such pain? At what point in my relatively short life had I gone off-script? As far back as I could remember, I had been a rule-follower. I had been unrelenting in my continual pursuit of perfection. What unwritten rule had I broken? "This isn't supposed to be happening to me," I whimpered as I lost consciousness.

The Flaming D

Instead of death that day, I had suffered a severe panic attack. Many days I contemplated suicide, but my love for my daughters blocked the fatal decision. I struggled to keep the remnants of the marriage together. When a glimmer of hope appeared, I retrieved my daughters from my parents and brought them home. I was doing everything humanly possible to keep this marriage from the brink of divorce. My husband's physical abuse had stopped, and I believed he was changing. Yet one fateful evening, I discovered that my husband was still seeing his mistress.

When I confronted him, rage replaced his humanity, and he slammed me against a wall. Something within me shattered. From the depths of my brokenness and pain, all the blackness in my soul erupted. With supernatural strength, I forced him out of the apartment and slammed the door. Then I crumpled to the floor in a broken heap.

Pulling myself together, I called my dad seeking solace, guidance, or just understanding. As I sobbed and emptied my heart, my father snapped, "Well, if you had listened to me, none of this would be happening."

Choking on the bile of rejection, I dropped the phone. No words can describe the sound of a shattering heart. There was nowhere to turn. There was no God of love. God was an angry and spiteful old man. My toxic companions screamed with glee.

A few months later, I was a divorced, single mother. A flaming *D* was branded on my forehead. My depth of shame could not be measured. I had committed one of the unpardonable sins. Angry god had placed me on a shelf, and I would no longer be effective in his master plan, whatever that was supposed to be. Adjusting to a new life, I resigned to live as a desolate woman.

Questioning everything I had been taught by my parents and the church led me down many dark alleys. Fortunately, visiting different churches introduced new perspectives on who God might be. I continued questioning his love. I thought I might have had the fire insurance of salvation, but a personal relationship with God or Jesus Christ was a foreign concept. My toxic companions were much more real than a personal God.

Exhaustion joined my horde of companions as I worked three jobs to survive. Four hours of sleep was a blessing. My daughters were the best part of my life, as were new friends that seemed to ignore my flaming *D*. Sometimes I wondered if those friends were really angels in disguise. I wasn't sure why God would take the time to send his angels my way, but I was thankful for each of them. Having angels temporarily join my growing host of companions was rather refreshing.

My Guardian Angel

One of my three jobs was delivering newspapers seven days a week, three hundred sixty-five days a year. I had to be at the paper drop by 4:00 a.m. Monday through Saturday in order to meet the delivery deadline of 5:30 a.m. On Sundays I had to be at the paper drop by midnight. Sunday mornings were extremely difficult. I had five hundred customers, and the size of the Sunday morning edition was so large, I had to make multiple trips in order to load and unload my car. To make that schedule work, I did not go to bed on Saturday nights.

I never really thought about how dangerous this job might be. I'm not sure I was naïve or just determined to do whatever I could to survive and take care of my daughters. I was young, physically strong, and determined. I had no idea I also had a handsome guardian angel.

One Saturday my daughters and I went to visit my former mother-in-law. After our visit, we came home late to discover that my apartment had been ransacked. My ex-husband had broken into my apartment, destroyed many of my belongings, and stole some jewelry. I called his mother, and then I called the police.

The policeman who took the report was very kind and attentive. He seemed to genuinely care about me and my daughters. After explaining my right to press charges and completing the necessary paperwork, the policeman turned to leave. After hesitating for a second, he informed me that he had been watching over me for several months as I delivered newspapers. I laughed. "So you are the cop car I see on a regular basis." His response was much more serious, "You do realize that being out that time of morning is not safe for a young attractive woman like yourself!" I just smiled.

As he walked toward his patrol car, he asked if I would mind him stopping by the paper drop later to check on me. I told him that was fine. My mother-in-law had arrived and agreed to spend the night so I wouldn't have to worry about taking the twins with me this time.

Not only did that policeman stop by the drop early that Sunday morning, he began visiting me every morning on a regular basis. I looked forward to his visits. For the first time in years, I felt a glimmer of happiness. He was strong, compassionate, and intelligent. He listened to me and seemed to value my opinions. I felt appreciated, and most of all, I felt protected. Of course, the uniform didn't hurt.

He made me feel beautiful, intelligent, and valuable. He was not only my protector early in the morning, he was also my protector at my job where I worked as a legal assistant. I had shared with him my discomfort with my boss making unwanted advances. My policeman gave me a photograph of himself in uniform. I placed his picture on my desk the next day. When my boss made his early morning visit to my desk, a policeman in full uniform was staring back at him. That photograph became a deterrent to a boss that had sexually harassed me for months.

As our friendship grew, I jumped out of bed early each morning so I would have more time to visit with my guardian angel. I no longer dreaded delivering those papers. The feeling of worthlessness was fading. I was falling in love. There was only one problem: he was married and had two children.

I didn't care. I loved him. I wanted to be with him. I felt alive when I was with him. How could this be wrong? I ignored the voice telling me to run. Instead, I fell head-over-heels into the arms of a married man. Guilt gnawed at my heart every time I thought about his wife and children. I was the other woman, the adulteress, the potential homewrecker. I had become the very woman I once hated. After several months, the guilt became too great. I broke up with my policeman.

He wrote me a beautiful letter encouraging me to believe in myself and start going after my dreams. For a few weeks, I would catch a glimpse of my guardian angel, but at some point, he asked to be reassigned to another beat. I never saw him again.

I was no longer the other woman, and I learned to hide the scarlet letter *A* rather well. While it might not have been visible to others, the *A* was seared into my bruised heart. I tried not to think about the fact that I had almost ruined another woman's marriage. How could I have been so irresponsible? My heart was too bruised and too vulnerable. My life would be better without the love of a man. I didn't need or want any more companions.

The Flaming DR

After two years as a single mother, my former brother-in-law introduced me to Carey, a friend of his. I was drawn to Carey's quiet strength and loving stability. He was kind, considerate, and compassionate. He loved my daughters, and they loved him. My bruised heart healed, and I allowed myself to love again. After dating four years, we married. My parents did not attend the wedding. I was now the daughter with *DR* scorched on her forehead—and the DR was not an abbreviation for doctor. Now that divorced and remarried were added to my identity, those familiar companions of fear, shame, and condemnation continued to stalk me.

My ex-husband relinquished his parental rights, and Carey adopted the twins. They were officially adopted on their tenth birthday. The next several years were filled with soccer, school events, and church attendance. Caring friends and healthy Christians proved to be instruments in thawing my wounded heart. One such couple was Bob and Priscilla Anderson.

Bob began pastoring the church we attended. I had never met anyone like those two. Bob's sense of humor surprised me more than anything. The preachers in my life had always been very serious. Bob loved life, and he loved Jesus. Bob and Priscilla's joyous glow melted some of the icy tentacles of bitterness in my heart.

Two years into Bob's pastorate, the church started having problems. Some were like those my dad had experienced years earlier. Like my parents, Bob and Priscilla were left penniless when they left the church. Yet their faith and courage challenged much of my unbelief.

Bob and Priscilla invited us to visit a church they had been attending. The church was considered one of the *mega* churches in Texas. Recovering from the shock of the size and number of people attending, my family settled into regular Sunday attendance.

A year passed, and Bob and Priscilla moved to start a ministry in California. In response to their urging, I joined a Bible study group. This decision opened the door to experiencing the true God of love. Our group began studying *Experiencing God* written by Henry Blackaby and Claude King. With every turn of the page, scales of unbelief fell from my heart. I discovered that I had been "practicing a sterile religion rather than enjoying a growing, vibrant, personal relationship with the living God" (Blackaby 2). Upon learning that God was more interested in a love relationship with me than he was in what I did for him, I surrendered my heart and life to my Creator God through his loving son, Jesus Christ (Blackaby 39). Digging deeper into God's word forced my toxic companions of fear, shame, and condemnation to retreat a few steps.

A year after completing the study, our son, Cody, was born. He was a joy to everyone. His sisters adored him. Even as a toddler, there were signs that he was going to be a little comedian. While life was not perfect and struggles continued, more angels joined my group of companions.

Confronting My Toxic Companions

In 2002 Carey was laid off from his job, and we moved to Alabama where he started working for his cousin. I started a job as a paralegal at high-profile law firm in Mobile. We joined a church near our home where I was accepted as a child of God. No one seemed to mind the *DR* tattooed on my forehead.

I began teaching Sunday school for divorced and remarried women and began speaking at ladies' retreats. Through prayer and Bible study, I began the long journey of making peace with my past. The truth of Romans 8:28 chipped away at my unhealthy relationship with my toxic traveling companions. "And we know that all things work together for good to them that love God, to them who are the called according to his purpose" (Rom. 8:28).

The year 2005 was a roller coaster. Both daughters married; my first grandchild was born; Hurricane Katrina hit; and my mother was diagnosed with renal cell carcinoma. Two weeks after removal of her left kidney, Mom became psychotic and was placed in a special institution to undergo electric shock therapy. I prayed endlessly that God would heal my mother. Some of the most vivid evidence of God's love flooded my life during that time; many are too sacred to share.

While the cancer did not spread, Mom struggled daily with mental illness. The doctors could not explain what caused this. Some speculated that anesthesia may have opened a door to the psychosis; no one knew for sure.

During my mother's continued fight against mental illness, my relationship with my parents healed. Accepting the truth of Ephesians

1:3–6 healed some of my brokenness. God had chosen me and loved me before speaking the world into existence. I was the daughter of the Creator God. His love for me was eternal.

> Blessed be the God and Father of our Lord Jesus Christ, who has blessed us in Christ with every spiritual blessing in the heavenly places, even as he chose us in him before the foundation of the world, that we should be holy and blameless before him. In love he predestined us for adoption to himself as sons through Jesus Christ, according to the purpose of his will, to the praise of his glorious grace, with which he has blessed us in the Beloved. (Eph. 1:3–6 English Standard Version)

My toxic companions seemed to be traveling at a safe distance.

In 2010, I felt led to finish my college degree. After researching and praying, the Lord led me to Liberty University Online. I was intimidated by the thought of going back to school after thirty-one years. Stuffing the fear, I dove in. I loved studying.

I continued to work full time and go to school full time. Without the Lord's strength and my husband's support, I would not have been able to reach that long-anticipated goal. Taking theology classes and digging deeper into God's word helped me grow spiritually. Love for writing was also unearthed. I felt compelled to share the love of God with others.

In 2012, on my fifty-third birthday, I graduated *summa cum laude* with a bachelor's degree in multidisciplinary studies. As I sat among the crowd of thirty-five thousand people, I listened to Dr. Falwell proudly explain how the online program was helping thousands of individuals around the world. Suddenly I heard him speak my name. He acknowledged my long journey to complete my degree. I was speechless. A wave of joy washed over me like nothing I had ever known. The DR on my forehead faded, and my toxic companions lagged farther behind.

Dumping Toxic Companions

In May of 2015, we discovered that the renal cell carcinoma had been hiding and slowly growing in my mother's brain and lungs. On June 6, 2015, Mom lost her battle with cancer. She stepped from her pain-ridden body into the presence of her Savior. One week later, my third grandchild was born.

Grief and joy form a curious relationship. One minute I was overwhelmed with grief, the next I was oozing with happiness. The stress of my job, Mom's death, and challenges in some of my relationships began eroding my ability to cope. My toxic companions were sneaking closer.

One year after Mom's death, I started meeting with a Christian counselor who was helping me peel back the layers of dysfunction. My counselor wisely identified my toxic companions as liars. We began the painful process of dumping them.

Shame had become a form of bondage that kept me imprisoned and separated from God's healing grace. Healing is painful. Ripping away years of woundedness and revealing the ugly pus wounds underneath is not a pleasant operation. My lifelong toxic companions had twisted so tightly around my woundedness that extracting them is physically painful.

As part of my healing process, I began reading *Present Over Perfect* by Shauna Niequist. I am stunned at how the Lord uses this book to continue softening my heart to his love. Shauna is a preacher's kid and a kindred spirit. I relate to many of her struggles.

My belief in my own worth, because of God's love, began to grow, like a just-lit candle—flickery and fragile at first, and then stronger, stronger. And over time that deep pool of unworthiness receded a little.

Another way to say it: I used to believe there was something wrong with me and love was a lie. Now I see love is truth and darkness is a lie. (Niequist 72)

While making changes and chipping away at some of the busyness in my life, I resigned from the ladies' ministry at church and from my chaplain ministry. These may appear to be strange decisions, but I am learning that God always has a better plan.

In the process of decluttering and healing, I began to think about sharing my story with others. Writing this book is my way of sharing. This part of my journey is also allowing healthy companions to replace the toxic ones.

Recently, while meditating on the cross, I had a renewed appreciation of the pain and shame Jesus suffered for me. As Jesus hung on the cross, he cried, "My God, my God, why have you forsaken me?" (Matt. 27:46 ESV). For the first time in eternity, God the Father separated himself from his son. Many of us think hell is just fire and brimstone, but hell is primarily total separation from God. God allowed his own son to suffer shame, become sin, and go to hell for *me*. "For our sake, he made him to be sin who knew no sin, so that in him we might become the righteousness of God" (2 Cor. 5:21 ESV). "Who for the joy that was set before him endured the cross, despising the shame, and is set down at the right hand of the throne of God" (Heb. 12:2 King James Version). This God of unfathomable love usurped the angry god I once feared.

Now when life gets a little crazy, I hear the distant whispers of my former companions, fear, shame, and condemnation. Thankfully, they are only distant whispers. I have dumped those toxic companions for the truth of God's word and his unfathomable love. The words of Jared C. Wilson echo my faith-journey:

> But here's the good news. That real you, the you inside that you hide, the you that you try to protect, the you that you hope nobody sees or knows—that's the you that God loves.
>
> No, he doesn't love your sin, of course. But he loves your true self. Without pretense, without façade, without image management, without the religious makeup. You the sinner, you the idolater, you the worshiper of false gods—that's the you Jesus loves.
>
> Look, this is the whole point of the Christian message: God loves sinners.
>
> Jesus died for sinners. He didn't wait for us to get our act together. (He knew we never could!) (Wilson 88).

If I could transport myself back in time, I would wrap my arms around that frightened little girl and whisper, "God loves you more than you can imagine. You are precious beyond compare."

> For I am convinced that neither death, nor life, nor angels, nor heavenly rulers, nor things that are present, nor things to come, nor powers, nor height, nor depth, nor anything else in creation will be able to separate us from the love of God in Christ Jesus our Lord. (Rom. 8:38–39 New English Translation)

Bibliography

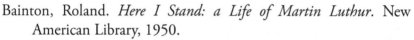

Bainton, Roland. *Here I Stand: a Life of Martin Luthur*. New American Library, 1950.

Blackaby, Henry, Richard Blackaby, and Claude King. *Experiencing God*. B&H Publishing Group, 2008.

Niequist, Shauna. *Present Over Perfect: Leaving Behind Frantic for a Simpler, More Soulful Way of Living*. Zondervan, 2016.

Wilson, Jared C. *The Imperfect Disciple: Grace for People Who Can't Get Their Act Together*. Baker Books, 2017.

About the Author

Kathy holds a BS in multidisciplinary studies from Liberty University. She is the president of Fervent Grace Ministries a nonprofit organization committed to proclaiming God's passionate, unconditional love and grace, encouraging an authentic relationship with Jesus Christ, and empowering women to develop transparent, grace-filled lives free from pretense and facade. Kathy is a former chaplain with Marketplace Chaplains and currently works as a litigation paralegal for a law firm in Daphne, Alabama. She is also a member of Jubilee Baptist Church in Daphne, where she enjoys teaching a great group of ladies affectionately known as Mixed Blessings. Kathy and her husband have three grown children, three grandchildren, and a sweet rescue dog named Bella. If Kathy isn't reading or writing, you will find her at the beach, in the mountains, or anywhere there's peace and quiet.

You can contact Kathy through her website at www.ferventgrace.org or email her at kmcinnis@ferventgrace.org.

CPSIA information can be obtained
at www.ICGtesting.com
Printed in the USA
BVHW081735140119
537772BV00009B/1327/P